States RHODE ISLAND

by Tyler Maine

CAPSTONE PRESS
a capstone imprint

Next Page Books are published by Capstone Press,
1710 Roe Crest Drive, North Mankato, Minnesota 56003
www.mycapstone.com

Library of Congress Cataloging-in-Publication Data
Cataloging-in-publication information is on file with the Library of
Congress.
ISBN 978-1-5157-0427-0 (library binding)
ISBN 978-1-5157-0486-7 (paperback)
ISBN 978-1-5157-0538-3 (ebook PDF)

Editorial Credits
Jaclyn Jaycox, editor; Kazuko Collins and Katy LaVigne, designers;
Morgan Walters, media researcher; Tori Abraham, production specialist

Photo Credits
Bridgeman Images: Bridgeman Images/Collection of the New-York
Historical Society, middle 18; Capstone Press: Angi Gahler, map 4, 7;
Corbis: David Duprey, 11; CriaImages.com: Jay Robert Nash Collection,
top 18; Dreamstime: Arenacreative, 10; Getty Images: New York
Daily News Archive, 28; Glow Images: H.-D. Falkenstein, bottom 18;
Newscom: AdMedia/Byron Purvis, bottom 19, MATTHEW HEALEY/UPI,
29, Picture History, middle 19, USA Today Sports/Joe Camporeale, top
19; North Wind Picture Archives, 25, 27; One Mile Up, Inc., flag, seal
23; Science Source: Dirk Wiersma, top left 21; Shutterstock: aleks-p,
bottom left 8, Annmarie Young, bottom 21, dolphfyn, middle right 21,
Enfi, 7, Everett Historical, 12, freya-photographer, top right 21, Garrett
Nantz, 9, Holly Kuchera, bottom left 20, IM_photo, cover, Jan Faukner,
14, Joy Brown, bottom right 8, 16, 17, Mariusz S. Jurgielewicz, top
left 20, Mary Terriberry, 26, mcdonojj, 6, Natalia Ganelin, top right 20,
Olga Lyubkina, bottom right 20, SDmitri Malyshev, bottom 24, Sean
Pavone, 5, Stephen B. Goodwin, 13, STUDIO GRAND OUEST, top 24,
William Warner, 15; Wikimedia: Alex Huck, middle left 21

All design elements by Shutterstock

Printed and bound in China.
0316/CA21600187
012016   009436F16

TABLE OF CONTENTS

Want to take your research further? Ask your librarian if your school subscribes to PebbleGo Next. If so, when you see this helpful symbol ⓀⓀ throughout the book, log onto www.pebblegonext.com for bonus downloads and information.

LOCATION

Rhode Island is one of the New England states. It's located in the northeast section of the United States. Massachusetts borders Rhode Island to the north and east. Connecticut lies to the west. Southern Rhode Island faces the Atlantic Ocean. Narragansett Bay cuts deeply into Rhode Island. It almost divides the state in two. This waterway is an arm of the Atlantic Ocean. At the head of the bay is Providence, the capital and largest city. Warwick and Cranston are the state's next largest cities.

PebbleGo Next Bonus!
To print and label
your own map, go to
www.pebblegonext.com
and search keywords:

RI MAP

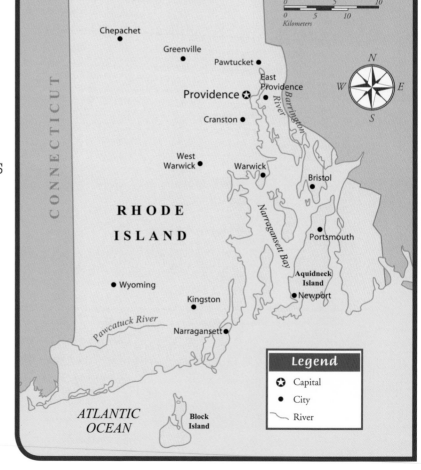

Scale
Miles
0   5   10
0   5   10
Kilometers

CONNECTICUT

Woonsocket

Chepachet

Greenville

Pawtucket

East Providence

Providence ✪

Barrington River

Cranston

West Warwick

Warwick

Bristol

RHODE ISLAND

Narragansett Bay

Portsmouth

Aquidneck Island

Wyoming

Kingston

Newport

Pawcatuck River

Narragansett

N
W   E
S

ATLANTIC OCEAN

Block Island

Legend
✪ Capital
• City
~ River

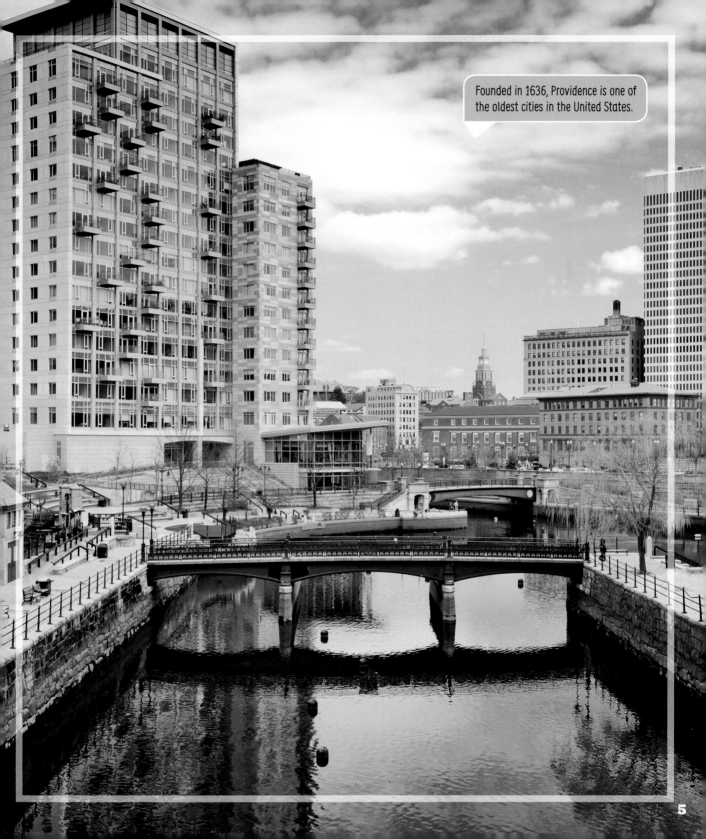

Founded in 1636, Providence is one of the oldest cities in the United States.

GEOGRAPHY

Rhode Island can be divided into the Coastal Lowlands and the Eastern New England Upland. The Coastal Lowlands includes land near Narragansett Bay and many islands. The region is made up of sandy beaches, low plains, and saltwater ponds. Some of the shoreline around the bay and islands has steep, rocky cliffs. The Eastern New England Upland covers the rest of the state. This region has gently rolling hills and valleys. Lakes, ponds, and reservoirs are also scattered throughout this region. The highest point in the state is Jerimoth Hill. It rises 812 feet (247 meters) above sea level in the western part of the Upland.

To watch a video about Slater Mill, go to www.pebblegonext.com and search keywords:

RI VIDEO

The Newport Bridge connects Newport on Aquidneck Island to Jamestown on Conanicut Island.

Point Judith Lighthouse is on the coast of southern Rhode Island in Narragansett.

Legend

- ▲ Highest Point
- ⬭ Lake
- ∿ River

▲ Jerimoth Hill

EASTERN NEW ENGLAND UPLAND

Blackstone River

Woonasquatucket River

Seekonk River

Providence River

Scituate Reservoir

Pawtuxet River

COASTAL LOWLANDS

Narragansett Bay

Sakonnet River

Aquidneck Island

N
W   E
S

Scale
Miles
0   5   10
0   5   10
Kilometers

Pawcatuck River

Worden Pond

Conanicut Island

Watchaug Pond

ATLANTIC OCEAN

Block Island

WEATHER

Temperatures in Rhode Island average around 29 degrees Fahrenheit (minus 2 degrees Celsius) in the winter and 71°F (22°C) in the summer. Breezes coming off the ocean and Narragansett Bay help control the temperature near the coast.

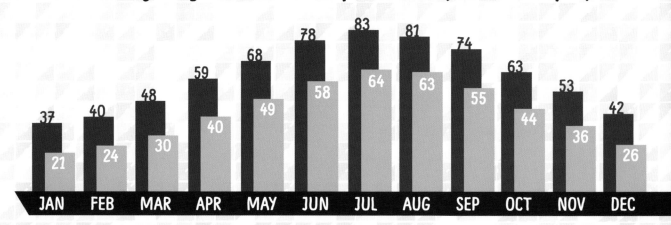

Average High and Low Temperatures (Providence, RI)

Month	High	Low
JAN	37	21
FEB	40	24
MAR	48	30
APR	59	40
MAY	68	49
JUN	78	58
JUL	83	64
AUG	81	63
SEP	74	55
OCT	63	44
NOV	53	36
DEC	42	26

The Breakers

The Breakers is a 70-room mansion in Newport built in 1895. The mansion is a National Historic Landmark.

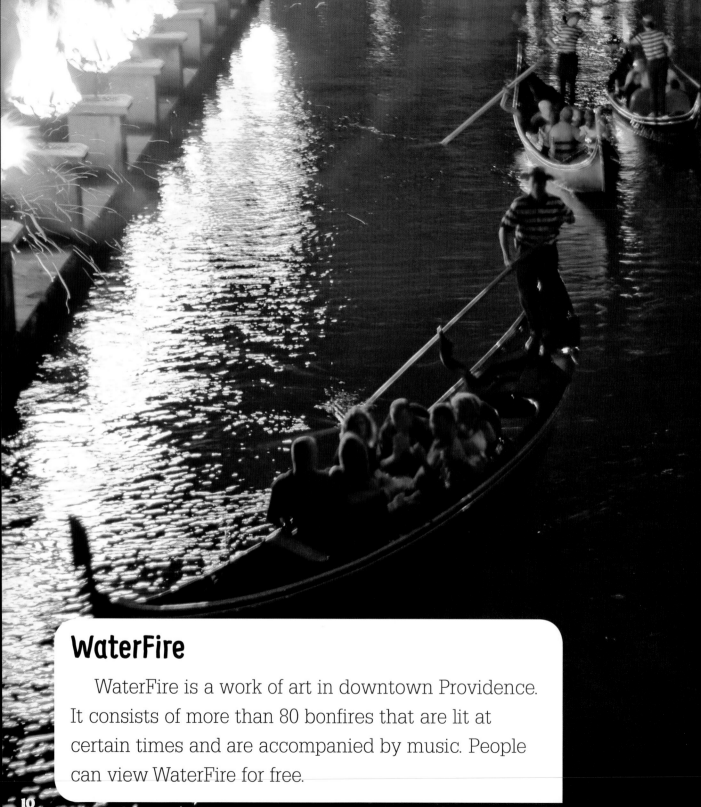

WaterFire

WaterFire is a work of art in downtown Providence.
It consists of more than 80 bonfires that are lit at
certain times and are accompanied by music. People
can view WaterFire for free.

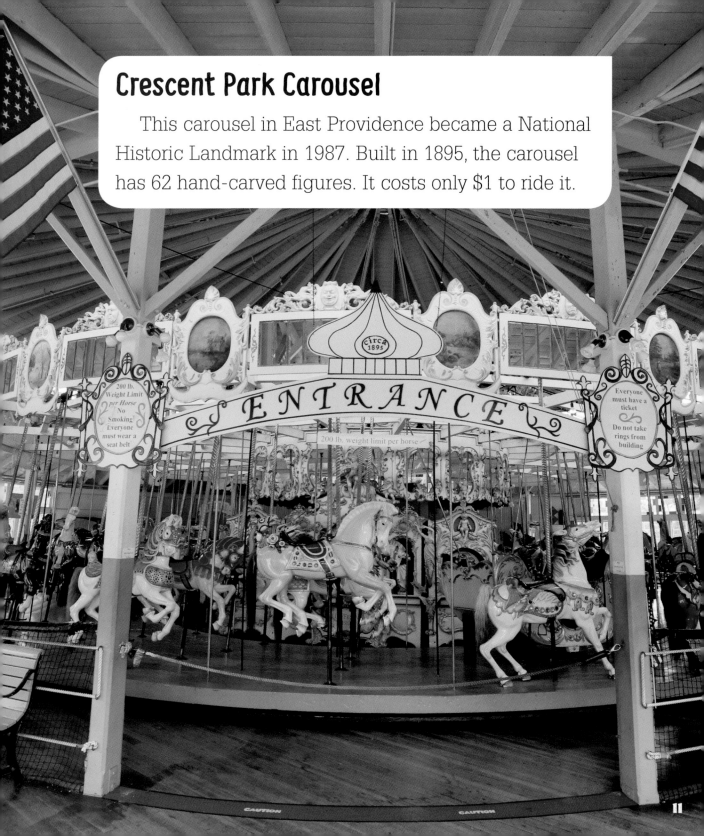

Crescent Park Carousel

This carousel in East Providence became a National Historic Landmark in 1987. Built in 1895, the carousel has 62 hand-carved figures. It costs only $1 to ride it.

Roger Williams was often a mediator between the American Indians and the colonies.

In 1636 Puritan minister Roger Williams established Providence, which was Rhode Island's first permanent settlement. Williams strongly believed in religious freedom and in treating American Indians fairly. Unfortunately settlers often clashed with their native neighbors. In 1676 settlers defeated the American Indians in King Philip's War.

On May 4, 1776, Rhode Island was the first colony to declare independence from Great Britain. After the colonists won the Revolutionary War, Rhode Island became the 13th state.

Rhode Island has three branches of government. The legislative branch makes the state laws. Lawmakers serve in the General Assembly. It has a 50-member Senate and a 100-member House of Representatives. The executive branch carries out the state's laws. The judicial branch is made up of judges and their courts. They decide whether someone has broken a law.

The statue of "The Independent Man" sits on top of the state capitol building.

INDUSTRY

Service industries, farming, manufacturing, and commercial fishing are all part of Rhode Island's diverse economy. Most Rhode Islanders work in the service industry. This industry includes jobs in tourism, health care, education, office work, sales, and government services. In recent years tourism has helped Rhode Island's economy. Sandy beaches, historic sites, and recreational activities attract many vacationers each year. Jewelry and silverware are Rhode Island's most common manufactured goods. The toy and game company Hasbro is based in Providence. Commercial fishing has been an important part of Rhode Island since colonial times.

Both costume and fine jewelry are produced in Rhode Island.

Commercial fishing boats are a common sight off the coast of Rhode Island.

POPULATION

About 75 percent of Rhode Islanders are white. Their immigrant ancestors came from a wide variety of European countries. The earliest settlers came mainly from England. In the 1820s large groups of Irish immigrants came to the United States in search of jobs. Another wave of immigration started in 1890. These immigrants came mostly from Italy. About 5 percent of Rhode Islanders are African-American. A small number of them descend from New England slaves of the 1700s. Most descend from freed Southern slaves.

Population by Ethnicity

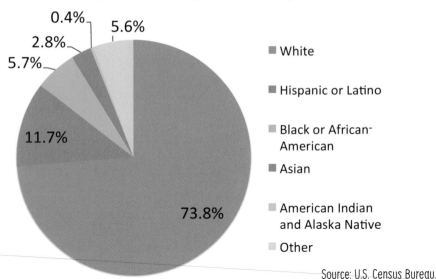

0.4%
2.8%
5.7%
5.6%
11.7%
73.8%

- White
- Hispanic or Latino
- Black or African-American
- Asian
- American Indian and Alaska Native
- Other

Source: U.S. Census Bureau.

Hispanics make up about 12 percent of Rhode Island's population. About 3 percent of Rhode Islanders are from Asia. A small number of American Indians also live in the state.

FAMOUS PEOPLE

George M. Cohan (1878–1942) was an actor and composer. He was famous for musical comedies. He wrote "Yankee Doodle Dandy" and "Give My Regards to Broadway." He was born in Providence.

Gilbert Stuart (1755–1828) was an artist. He painted the famous portrait of George Washington that now appears on the United States' one-dollar bill. He was born in Saunderstown.

Roger Williams (circa 1603–1683) was the Puritan leader who founded Rhode Island. He was born in England.

Paul Konerko (1976–) played Major League Baseball from 1997 to 2014. He was born in Providence.

Samuel Slater (1768–1835) earned the nickname the Father of American Industry. He built Rhode Island's first water-powered textile mill in Pawtucket. He was born in England.

Robert Capron (1998–) stars in the *Diary of a Wimpy Kid* movies. He was born in Providence.

STATE SYMBOLS

Tree

red maple

Flower

violet

Bird

Rhode Island red

Fish

striped bass

PebbleGo Next Bonus! To make Johnnycakes, a long-time Rhode Island tradition, go to www.pebblegonext.com and search keywords:

RI RECIPE

Mineral

bowenite

Fruit

Rhode Island greening apple

Rock

cumberlandite

Drink

coffee milk

Shell

quahog

FAST FACTS

STATEHOOD
1790

CAPITAL ☆
Providence

LARGEST CITY •
Providence

SIZE
1,034 square miles (2,678 square kilometers)
land area (2010 U.S. Census Bureau)

POPULATION
1,050,511 (2013 U.S. Census estimate)

STATE NICKNAME
Ocean State

STATE MOTTO
"Hope"

STATE SEAL

The state seal was officially adopted in 1896. The seal has an anchor in the center. The word "Hope" is the state motto. The year 1636 is on the bottom along the border. Roger Williams founded Providence in that year. Around the rest of the border are the words "Seal of the State of Rhode Island and Providence Plantations."

PebbleGo Next Bonus!
To print and color
your own flag, go to
www.pebblegonext.com
and search keywords:

RI FLAG

STATE FLAG

Rhode Island's flag has a white background. A gold anchor in the center represents hope. Thirteen gold stars form a circle around the anchor. The stars stand for the 13 original colonies. A blue ribbon under the anchor has the state's motto, "Hope," in gold letters. Rhode Island adopted its flag in 1897.

MINING PRODUCTS

sand and gravel, gemstones, granite, limestone

MANUFACTURED GOODS

jewelry, silverware, chemicals, metal products, plastics and rubber products, computer and electronic equipment

FARM PRODUCTS

greenhouse and nursery plants, potatoes, corn, hay, apples

PebbleGo Next Bonus!
To learn the lyrics to
the state song, go to
www.pebblegonext.com
and search keywords:
RI SONG

RHODE ISLAND TIMELINE

1500s
Several American Indian groups, including the Narragansetts, Wampanoags, Niantics, Pequots, and Nipmucs, live in the area of Rhode Island.

1524
Italian explorer Giovanni da Verrazano first sails into Narragansett Bay.

1620
The Pilgrims establish a colony in the New World in present-day Massachusetts.

1636
Puritan minister Roger Williams founds Providence.

1647 The settlements of Providence, Newport, Warwick, and Portsmouth unite to form one colony.

1776 On May 4 Rhode Island officially declares independence from Great Britain.

1790 Rhode Island becomes the 13th state on May 29.

1790 Slater Mill is founded in Pawtucket by Samuel Slater. It is the first successful water-powered cotton mill in America.

1843
On May 2 Rhode Island becomes the first state where African-Americans can vote.

1861–1865
The Union and the Confederacy fight the Civil War. Rhode Island soldiers fight with the Union.

1900
Providence becomes Rhode Island's official state capital.

1914–1918
World War I is fought; the United States enters the war in 1917.

1924

Henry and Helal Hassenfeld start the Hasbro toy and game company in Providence.

1938

On September 21 the Great New England Hurricane of 1938 causes $100 million in damage and more than 317 deaths in Rhode Island.

1939–1945

World War II is fought; the United States enters the war in 1941.

1969
Workers finish Interstate 95 and the Newport Bridge over Narragansett Bay.

1980
Claudine Schneider becomes the state's first woman to serve in Congress. She serves five terms in the U.S. House of Representatives.

2010
Rainstorms cause flooding and force thousands from their homes; property damage totals more than $200 million.

2015
Construction begins on the country's first offshore windfarm near Block Island.

Glossary

ancestor *(AN-ses-tuhr)*—a member of a person's family who lived a long time ago

clash *(KLASH)*—to fight or argue aggressively

descend *(dee-SEND)*—if you are descended from someone, you belong to a later generation of the same family

executive *(ig-ZE-kyuh-tiv)*—the branch of government that makes sure laws are followed

immigrant *(IM-uh-gruhnt)*—someone who comes from abroad to live permanently in a country

industry *(IN-duh-stree)*—a business which produces a product or provides a service

judicial *(joo-DISH-uhl)*—to do with the branch of government that explains and interprets the laws

legislature *(LEJ-iss-lay-chur)*—a group of elected officials who have the power to make or change laws for a country or state

mansion *(MAN-shuhn)*—a large, expensive house

reservoir *(REZ-ur-vor)*—a natural or artificial holding area for storing a large amount of water

tourism *(TOOR-i-zuhm)*—the business of taking care of visitors to a country or place

Read More

Felix, Rebecca. *What's Great About Rhode Island?* Our Great States. Minneapolis: Lerner Publications Company, 2015.

Ganeri, Anita. *United States of America: A Benjamin Blog and His Inquisitive Dog Guide.* Country Guides. Chicago: Heinemann Raintree, 2015.

Kleinmartin, Hex. *Rhode Island.* It's My State! New York: Cavendish Square Publishing, 2015.

Internet Sites

FactHound offers a safe, fun way to find Internet sites related to this book. All of the sites on FactHound have been researched by our staff.

Here's all you do:

Visit *www.facthound.com*

Type in this code: 9781515704270

Super-cool stuff! Check out projects, games and lots more at
www.capstonekids.com

Critical Thinking Using the Common Core

1. Who established the first permanent settlement, Providence, in Rhode Island? (Key Ideas and Details)

2. Name three landmarks that bring tourists to Rhode Island. (Key Ideas and Details)

3. Lakes, ponds, and reservoirs are scattered throughout Rhode Island. What is a reservoir? (Craft and Structure)

Index

31901062702016